Lightning
Bolt
Books™

Eerie Haunted Houses

Candice Ransom

Lerner Publications ◆ Minneapolis

Lerner Publications Company
An imprint of Lerner Publishing Group, Inc.
241 First Avenue North
Minneapolis, MN 55401 USA

For reading levels and more information, look up this title at www.lernerbooks.com.

Main body text set in Billy Infant regular.
Typeface provided by SparkType.

Editor: Alison Lorenz

Library of Congress Cataloging-in-Publication Data

Names: Ransom, Candice F., 1952- author.
Title: Eerie haunted houses / Candice Ransom.
Description: Minneapolis : Lerner Publications, 2021. | Series: Lightning bolt books—Spooked! | Includes bibliographical references and index. | Audience: Ages 6-9 | Audience: Grades 2-3 | Summary: "Send shivers up your spine with tales of spooky houses and the ghosts rumored to haunt them. You'll learn all about ghosts, the people who hunt them, real close encounters, and more!"— Provided by publisher.
Identifiers: LCCN 2019040543 (print) | LCCN 2019040544 (ebook) | ISBN 9781541596887 (library binding) | ISBN 9781728400488 (ebook)
Subjects: LCSH: Haunted houses—Juvenile literature. | Ghosts—Juvenile literature.
Classification: LCC BF1475 .R36 2020 (print) | LCC BF1475 (ebook) | DDC 133.1/22—dc23

LC record available at https://lccn.loc.gov/2019040543
LC ebook record available at https://lccn.loc.gov/2019040544

Manufactured in the United States of America
1-47794-48234-11/18/2019

Table of Contents

What Are Haunted Houses?

The old house has been empty for years. Cobwebs drape the corners. Dust covers the floor. *Thump-thump* goes the sound of footsteps on the stairs.

Stories about haunted houses go back thousands of years.

A doorknob slowly turns. The door creaks open. A misty shape seems to creep into the room. **Is it a ghost?**

Strange sounds can make it seem as though someone—or something—is walking around a house.

People sometimes hear strange sounds or see strange sights in old houses. They claim the spirits of those who died there haunt these houses.

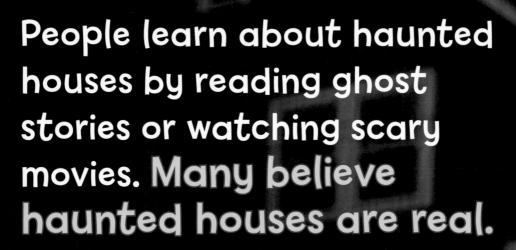

People learn about haunted houses by reading ghost stories or watching scary movies. Many believe haunted houses are real.

Have you heard a scary story?

The First Haunted House

Two thousand years ago in Greece, the author Pliny wrote a letter to a friend. He described a large house that had been empty for years. Then a man moved into the house.

According to Pliny's story, after the man found the skeleton, he never saw the ghost again.

One night, the man saw a ghost with chains around his hands and feet. The ghost led the man outside and then disappeared. The man dug up that spot and found a skeleton bound in chains.

Catch That Ghost!

Pliny's letter is one of the first records of a haunted house. People have often wondered if old, empty houses are haunted.

TV shows about haunted houses are popular. Many people watch these shows to see if houses are truly haunted.

Why do we watch scary shows? Sometimes it's fun to be scared!

Some people claim they are living in a haunted house. Sometimes, they let ghost hunters check out their home.

Ghost hunters speak with homeowners to find out more about the house's history.

Ghost hunters take videos to search for ghosts on the footage.

Ghost-hunting teams use special gear. They place microphones in empty rooms to pick up strange sounds. They use thermometers to check for cold spots where they think ghosts may be.

Sometimes photographs show odd, fuzzy shapes. Ghost hunters may say this is evidence that a place is haunted.

But TV shows about ghosts are not usually filmed in real time. The show often follows a script written before filming. This makes shows about hauntings less believable.

Most of the time, ghost hunters are really actors speaking prewritten lines.

Are Haunted Houses Real?

Some strange happenings can be explained. Old houses often have noisy pipes or squeaky floors. Those noises could be mistaken for footsteps.

Cold air can slip through windows. Odd figures in photographs could be dust reflected in a camera flash.

Can you think of other explanations for strange sounds and sights?

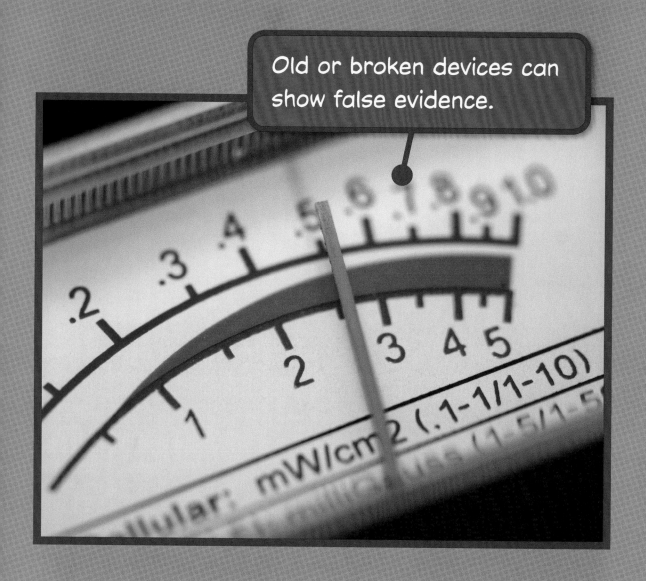

Old or broken devices can show false evidence.

Modern devices collect evidence. But untrained people often use these devices. Only professionals know how to understand the evidence that devices gather.

So far, no scientific evidence proves that haunted houses are real. But we can still enjoy stories and movies about them!

It's fun to tell scary stories—but not too scary!

Close Encounter

Can trains be haunted too? President Abraham Lincoln died on April 15, 1865. A train carried  his body from Washington, DC, to Springfield, Illinois. The train passed through Albany, New York. Years later, railroad workers in Albany saw a train draped in black. Skeletons in uniforms walked beside the cars. Some said the ghost train passed by at midnight every April 25—the same date the train carried Lincoln's body through the city.

Terrifying Trivia

- Almost half of Americans believe haunted houses are real. About one-fifth say they have seen a ghost.

- Some say that cats and dogs can sense haunted places.

- Most cultures have stories of ghosts and haunted buildings.

- Houses might be the most haunted places, but hospitals, prisons, hotels, churches, and other places might be haunted too.

Glossary

device: a machine or a tool that helps locate ghosts

evidence: proof that something may be true

haunt: to visit often or live in a place as a ghost

microphone: an instrument that records sound

professional: a trained person who earns money doing a job

real time: the actual time when something happens

script: the written text of a stage play, movie, or TV show

spirit: an energy inside living things believed to be bodiless and sometimes visible

thermometer: a tool that measures temperature

Further Reading

Brody, Walt. *Spooky Ghost Ships.* Minneapolis: Lerner Publications, 2021.

Ghost Facts for Kids: Kiddle Encyclopedia https://kids.kiddle.co/Ghost

"How to Make a Haunted House": Kidzworld https://www.kidzworld.com/article/26135-how -to-make-a-haunted-house

Rudolph, Jessica. *Ghost Houses.* New York: Bearport, 2017.

Tieck, Sarah. *Ghosts.* Minneapolis: Big Buddy Books, 2016.

Index

Photo Acknowledgments

Image credits: StephanieFrey/iStock/Getty Images, p. 2; SEAN GLADWELL/Getty Images, p. 4; nespyxel/Getty Images, p. 5; urbazon/Getty Images, p. 6; XiXinXing/istock/Getty Images, p. 7; EvrenKalinbacak/iStock/Getty Images, p. 8; Svetislav1944/Shutterstock.com, p. 9; Malcolm MacGregor/Getty Images, p. 10; Filograph/iStock/Getty Images, p. 11; Peter Kim/Shutterstock.com, p. 12; eddtoro/Shutterstock.com, p. 13; zef art/Shutterstock.com, p. 14; Lautaro Federico/Shutterstock.com, p. 15; Petr Lenz/Getty Images, p. 16; Ross Gordon Henry/Shutterstock.com, p. 17; scotspencer/Getty Images, p. 18; Westend61/Getty Images, pp. 19, 23; National Archives/Stocktrek Images/Getty Images, p. 20.

Cover images: oleshko andrey/Shutterstock.com; Razvan Ionut Dragomirescu/Shutterstock.com.